国际财务报告准则

《国际会计准则第28号——在联营企业和合营企业中的投资》

（汉英对照）

中国会计准则委员会　组织翻译

中国财政经济出版社

图书在版编目（CIP）数据

国际会计准则．第28号，在联营企业和合营企业中的投资：汉、英／中国会计准则委员会组织翻译．北京：中国财政经济出版社，2012.12

（国际财务报告准则）

ISBN 978－7－5095－4150－0

Ⅰ．①国…　Ⅱ．①中…　Ⅲ．①国际会计准则－汉、英　Ⅳ．①F233.1

中国版本图书馆CIP数据核字（2012）第287290号

责任编辑：樊清玉　　版式设计：康普宝蓝

封面设计：九州迅驰

中国财政经济出版社出版

URL：http：//ckfz.cfeph.cn

E－mail：ckfz@cfeph.cn

社址：北京市海淀区阜成路甲28号　邮政编码：100142

发行处电话：88190406　财经书店电话：64033436

河北零五印刷厂印刷　各地新华书店经销

787×1092毫米　16开　4.25印张　80 000字

2013年1月第1版　2013年1月河北第1次印刷

定价：16.00元

ISBN 978－7－5095－4150－0/F·3370

（图书出现印装问题，本社负责调换）

图字：01－2013－0578

本社质量投诉电话：010－88190744

International Financial Reporting Standards (IFRSs) together with their accompanying documents are issued by the International Accounting Standards Board (IASB):

30 Cannon Street, London, EC4M 6XH, United Kingdom.

Tel: +44 (0) 20 7246 6410   Fax: +44 (0) 20 7246 6411

Email: info@ifrs.org   Web: www.ifrs.org

ISBN 978-7-5095-4150-0

IFRS Foundation Publications Department

30 Cannon Street, London, EC4M 6XH, United Kingdom.

Tel: +44 (0) 20 7332 2730   Fax: +44 (0) 20 7332 2749

Email: publications@ifrs.org   Web: www.ifrs.org

国际财务报告准则（IFRSs）及其配套文件由国际会计准则理事会（IASB）发布。
30 Cannon Street, London, EC4M 6XH, United Kingdom.
Tel: +44 (0) 20 7246 6410　　Fax: +44 (0) 20 7246 6411
Email: info@ifrs.org
Web: www.ifrs.org

ISBN 978-7-5095-4150-0

国际财务报告准则中文翻译审核专家组

出版说明

2011年，国际会计准则理事会先后发布了《国际财务报告准则第10号——合并财务报表》、《国际财务报告准则第11号——合营安排》、《国际财务报告准则第12号——在其他主体中权益的披露》和《国际财务报告准则第13号——公允价值计量》四项新准则，并对《国际会计准则第1号——财务报表列报》、《国际会计准则第19号——雇员福利》、《国际会计准则第27号——合并财务报表和单独财务报表》和《国际会计准则第28号——在联营企业和合营企业中的投资》四项准则进行了修订。除修订后的《国际会计准则第1号》于2012年7月1日生效外，上述其他新发布或修订的国际财务报告准则都将于2013年1月1日起生效。

我国2006年发布的企业会计准则体系实现了与国际财务报告准则的趋同。2010年，财政部又发布了《中国企业会计准则与国际财务报告准则持续趋同路线图》。为借鉴国际财务报告准则完善我国企业会计准则体系，实现中国准则与国际财务报告准则的持续趋同，中国会计准则委员会组织人员对国际会计准则理事会新发布或修订的上述八项准则进行了翻译。经国际财务报告准则基金会认可的中文翻译审核专家组审核，上述国际财务报告准则中文版是国际财务报告准则基金会认可的国际财务报告准则官方译本，为国际财务报告准则基金会的正式出版物。

在翻译审校过程中，财政部会计司陆建桥、高大平、朱琳、陈瑜、夏文贤、徐华新、林屾等同志对本书的译稿进行了校译。财政部会计司副司长、中国会计学会秘书长刘光忠和财政部会计司司长、中国会计准则委员会秘书长杨敏对全部译稿进行了审阅。本书最后由财政部部长助理余蔚平和财政部党组副书记、副部长、中国会计准则委员会主席王军审定。值此相关国际财务报告准则中文版出版之际，特别感谢国际财务报告准则中文翻译审核专家组以及中国财政经济出版社的有关同志为本书的翻译出版工作所付出的辛勤劳动！

中国会计准则委员会

2013 年 1 月

目　　录

段落

引 言 …… 1－11

国际会计准则第28号——在联营企业和合营企业中的投资

目 标 …… 1

范 围 …… 2

定 义 …… 3－4

重大影响 …… 5－9

权益法 …… 10－15

权益法的运用 …… 16－43

豁免应用权益法 …… 17－19

分类为持有待售 …… 20－21

终止采用权益法 …… 22－24

所有者权益的变动 …… 25

权益法程序 …… 26－39

减值损失 …… 40－43

单独财务报表 …… 44

生效日期和过渡性规定 …… 45－46

参照《国际财务报告准则第9号》 …… 46

《国际会计准则第28号》（2003）的撤销 …… 47

理事会批准2003年12月发布的《国际会计准则第28号》

《国际会计准则第28号——在联营企业和合营企业中的投资》结论基础

不同意见

对照表

《国际会计准则第28号——在联营企业和合营企业中的投资》由第1段至47段组成。所有段落具有同等效力，但国际会计准则理事会在采纳本准则时保留了原国际会计准则委员会的段落格式。《国际会计准则第28号》应当结合结论基础、《国际财务报告准则前言》和《财务报告概念框架》一并阅读。在缺乏明确指南的情况下，《国际会计准则第8号——会计政策、会计估计变更和差错》提供了选择和应用会计政策的基础。

引言

1.《国际会计准则第 28 号——在联营企业和合营企业中的投资》规范了对联营企业中投资的会计处理，并明确了应用权益法对联营企业和合营企业中的投资进行会计处理的要求。

2. 本准则适用于自 2013 年 1 月 1 日或以后日期开始的年度期间。允许提前采用。

本准则的主要特征

3.《国际会计准则第 28 号》（2011 年修改）适用于所有对被投资者具有共同控制或重大影响的投资者。

4. 本准则将重大影响定义为参与被投资者的财务和经营政策决策的权力，但不是控制或共同控制这些政策。

5.《国际财务报告准则第 11 号——合营安排》规定了有关合营安排各参与方财务报告的原则。《国际财务报告准则第 11 号》将共同控制定义为按合同约定分享对一项安排的控制权，并且仅在对相关活动的决策要求分享控制权的参与方一致同意时才存在。

6. 主体采用《国际财务报告准则第 11 号》确定其参与的合营安排类型。一旦主体确定其在合营企业中拥有权益，主体应当确认一项投资，并根据《国际会计准则第 28 号》（2011 年修改）采用权益法对其进行会计处理，除非按照本准则规定主体豁免采用权益法。

权益法

7. 本准则将权益法定义为以成本对联营企业或合营企业的投资进行初始确认，并在取得日后投资者的权益包括其在被投资者损益中的份额，投资者的其他综合收益包括其在被投资者其他综合收益中的份额。

8. 主体在合并财务报表中采用权益法对其在联营企业和合营企业中的投资进行会计处理。没有子公司的主体也会使用权益法在财务报表中对其在联营企业和合营企业中的投资进行会计处理，尽管该财务表不能称为合并财务报表。主体唯一不采用权益法进行会计处理的财务报表是主体根据《国际会计准则第 27 号——单独财务报表》编制的单独财务报表。

豁免应用权益法

9. 本准则提供了豁免应用权益法的规定，类似于《国际财务报告准则第 10 号——合并财务报表》豁免母公司编制合并财务报表的规定。

10. 当联营企业或合营企业中的投资被风险资本组织、共同基金、信托公司和包括投连险基金在内的类似主体持有或间接持有时，本准则规定可以豁免应用权益法。这些投资可以根据《国际财务报告准则第 9 号——金融工具》以公允价值计量且其变动计入损益。

披露

11. 主体对被投资者具有共同控制或重大影响的披露要求，由《国际财务报告准则第 12 号——在其他主体中权益的披露》予以规范。

《国际会计准则第 28 号——在联营企业和合营企业中的投资》

目标

1. 本准则的目标是，规范在联营企业中投资的会计处理，并明确应用权益法对在联营企业和合营企业中的投资进行会计处理的要求。

范围

2. 本准则适用于所有对被投资者具有共同控制或重大影响的投资者。

定义

3. 本准则使用的下列术语，其含义为：

联营企业，指投资者对其具有重大影响的主体。

合并财务报表，指集团编制的财务报表，在该报表中母公司和子公司的资产、负债、所有者权益、收入、费用和现金流量都作为单一经济主体进行列报。

权益法，指以成本对投资进行初始确认，之后根据投资者享有的被投资者净资产份额的变动对其进行调整的会计处理方法。投资者的损益包括其在被投资者的损益中的份额，投资者的其他综合收益包括其在被投资者的其他综合收益中的份额。

合营安排，指两个或两个以上的参与方共同控制的一项安排。

共同控制，指按合同约定分享对一项安排的控制权，并且仅在对相关活动的决策要求分享控制权的参与方一致同意时才存在。

合营企业，指共同控制一项安排的参与方对该安排的净资产享有权利的合营安排。

合营者，指对合营企业具有共同控制的合营企业参与方。

重大影响，指参与被投资者的财务和经营政策决策的权力，但不是控制或共同控制这些政策。

4. 以下术语在《国际会计准则第 27 号——单独财务报表》第 4 段、《国际财务报告准则第 10 号——合并财务报表》附录一中予以定义，在本准则中使用的这些术语含义与上述国际财务报告准则中的定义相同：

- 对被投资者的控制
- 集团
- 母公司
- 单独财务报表
- 子公司

重大影响

5. 如果主体直接或间接地（例如通过子公司）持有被投资者 20% 或 20% 以上的表决权，即认为主体具有重大影响，除非能够明确证明情况并非如此。相反，如果主体直接或间接（例如通过子公司）持有被投资者 20% 以下的表决权，即认为主体不具有重大影响，除非能够明确证明存在这种影响。被投资者的绝大部分或大部分所有权被另一投资者拥有，并不排除主体对其具有重大影响。

6. 主体具有重大影响，通常由下列一种或多种方式证实：

（1）在被投资者董事会或类似权力机构中的代表；

（2）政策制定过程的参与情况，包括股利分配或其他分配决策的参与情况；

（3）主体与被投资者之间的重大交易；

（4）管理人员的交换；或者

（5）关键技术信息的提供。

7. 主体可能拥有认股权证、股票看涨期权、可转换为普通股的债务或权益工具或其他类似工具，如果执行或转换这些工具，将有可能赋予该主体对另一主体财务或经营决策的额外表决权，或减少其他主体的表决权（即潜在表决权）。在评估主体是否具有重大影响时，需要考虑目前存在的可执行或可转换的潜在表决权（包括由其他主体持有的潜在表决权）及其影响。例如，当潜在表决权直到将来某一日期或直到将来发生某一事项才能执行或转换时，该潜在表决权就不是当前可执行或可转换的。

8. 主体在评估潜在表决权是否有助于形成重大影响时，需要考量影响潜在表决权的所有事实和情况（包括行使潜在表决权的条件以及任何需要单独或是共同考虑的其他合同约定），但不包括管理层的意图以及执行或转换这些潜在表决权的财务能力。

9. 当主体不再具有参与被投资者的财务和经营政策决策的权力时，该主体就丧失了对被投资者的重大影响。例如，当联营企业被政府、法院、管理部门或监管机构控制时，就有可能发生上述情况。合同安排也可能导致上述情况的发生。

权益法

10. 在权益法下，以成本对联营企业或合营企业的投资进行初始确认；取得日以后，通过增加或减少投资的账面金额确认投资者在被投资者损益中应占的份额。投资者享有的被投资者的损益份额确认为投资者的损益。收到被投资者的分配，则冲减其投资的账面金额。被投资者其他综合收益的变动导致投资者对被投资者权益份额的变动，也可能需要调整其投资的账面金额。这类变动包括不动产、厂场和设备的重估，以及外币折算差额引起的变动。投资者所享有的这些变动的份额确认为投资者的其他综合收益（参见《国际会计准则第 1 号——财务报表列报》）。

11. 如果收到的分配与联营企业或合营企业的业绩几乎不相关，投资者根据收到的分配确认的收益可能不足以计量对联营企业或合营企业投资所赚取的收益。由于投资者对被投资者具有共同控制或重大影响，投资者对联营企业或合营企业的业绩拥有权益，从而拥有其投资回报。投资者通过扩展其财务报表的范围，以包含其分享的被投资者损益份额，对这一权益进行会计处理。因此，权益法的应用提供了关于投资者净资产和损益的更多信息。

12. 当存在潜在表决权或包含潜在表决权的其他衍生工具时，主体对联营企业或合营企业的权益仅取决于现有的所有者权益，并不反映可能执行或转换的潜在表决权和其他衍生工具，除非第 13 段适用。

13. 在一些情况下，由于某项交易使主体目前能够获得与所有者权益相关的回报，则该主体实质上拥有所有权。在这样的情况下，确定分配给主体的比例应当考虑目前能使主体获得相关回报的潜在表决权和其他衍生工具的最终行权。

14. 《国际财务报告准则第 9 号——金融工具》不适用于采用权益法进行会计处理的在联营企业和合营企业中的权益。当包含潜在表决权的金融工具实质上目前能够使主体获得与其在联营企业和合营企业中的所有者权益相关的回报时，该金融工具不适用《国际财务报告准则第 9 号》。在其他情况下，包含在联营企业或合营企业中潜在表决权的金融工具应当按照《国际财务报告准则第 9 号》进行会计处理。

15. 除非联营企业或合营企业中的一项投资或其中部分投资根据《国际财务报告准则第 5 号——持有待售的非流动资产和终止经营》分类为持有待售，否则该项投资或其中未被分类为持有待售的剩余权益，应分类为非流动资产。

权益法的应用

16. 对被投资者具有共同控制或重大影响的主体应采用权益法对联营企业或合营企业中的投资进行会计处理，除非该投资符合第 17 段至 19 段的豁免规定。

豁免应用权益法

17. 主体如果是根据《国际财务报告准则第 10 号》第 4 段（1）豁免编制合并财务报表的母公司或者符合下列所有条件，则不需要对联营企业或合营企业中的投资应用权益法：

（1）主体是另一主体的全资或者非全资子公司，并且主体的其他所有者（包括没有表决权的所有者）已被告知且不反对主体不应用权益法。

（2）主体的债务或权益工具没有在公开市场（国内或国外的证券交易所或者，包括当地或地区性市场的柜台交易市场）上交易。

（3）主体没有为了在公开市场发行任何类型的工具，而向证券交易委员会或其他监管机构报送过和正在报送财务报表。

（4）主体的最终母公司或任一中间母公司按照国际财务报告准则编制可供公开使用的合并财务报表。

18. 当联营企业或合营企业中的投资被风险资本组织、共同基金、信托公司和包括投连险基金在内的类似主体持有或间接持有时，主体可以根据《国际财务报告准则第 9 号》对联营企业和合营企业中的投资选择以公允价值计量且其变动计入损益。

19. 当主体在联营企业中的投资有一部分是通过风险资本组织、共同基金、信托公司或包括投连险基金在内的类似主体间接持有时，无论该风险资本组织、共同基金、信托公司和包括投连险基金在内的类似主体是否对这部分投资具有重大影响，主体都可以根据《国际财务报告准则第 9 号》对联营企业中的这部分投资选择以公允价值计量且其变动计入损益。如果主体作了这样的选择，主体应对投资中未通过风险资本组织、共同基金、信托公司和包括投连险基金在内的类似主体持有的剩余部分应用权益法。

分类为持有待售

20. 主体应对符合持有待售条件的联营企业和合营企业中的投资或部分投资应用《国际财务报告准则第 5 号》。在处置分类为持有待售的那部分投资之前，对联营企业和合营企业中未被分类为持有待售的剩余投资部分应采用权益法进行会计处理。处置发生后，主体应根据《国际财务报告准则第 9 号》对联营企业或合营企业中的剩余权益进行会计处理，除非剩余权益继续归属于适用权益法的联营企业或合营企业投资。

21. 当之前划分为持有待售的联营企业和合营企业中的投资或部分投资不再符合这种分类条件时，该投资应从被分类为持有待售之日开始追溯采用权益法进行会计处理。分类为持有待售期间的财务报表应作相应调整。

终止采用权益法

22. 当主体的投资不再是联营企业或合营企业时，主体应按照下列要求终止采用权益法：

（1）如果该投资成为子公司，主体应根据《国际财务报告准则第 3 号——企业合并》和《国际财务报告准则第 10 号》对该投资进行会计处理。

（2）如果原联营企业或合营企业的剩余权益是金融资产，主体应以公允价值计量该剩余权益。剩余权益的公允价值应视为根据《国际财务报告准则第 9 号》对金融资产进行初始确认的公允价值。主体应将以下两者的差异计入损益：

①剩余权益的公允价值和联营企业或合营企业中部分权益的处置收入；和

②终止采用权益法时该投资的账面金额。

（3）当主体终止采用权益法时，对于以前确认为其他综合收益的所有与该投资有关的金额，主体应当采用与被投资者直接处置相关资产或负债相同的基础进行会计处理。

23. 因此，如果被投资者以前在其他综合收益确认的利得或损失，在处置相关资产或负债时被重分类至损益，则主体在终止采用权益法时将利得或损失从权益重新分类至损益（作为重分类调整）。例如，如果联营企业或合营企业存在与境外经营有关的累积汇兑差额，并且该主体终止采用权益法，则该主体应将以前在其他综合收益中确认的、与境外经营有关的利得或损失重分类至损益。

24. 如果联营企业中的投资变成合营企业中的投资，或者合营企业中的投资变成联营企业中的投资，主体继续应用权益法，不再重新计量剩余权益。

所有者权益的变动

25. 当主体在联营企业或合营企业中的所有者权益减少了，但该主体仍应用权益法时，如果在处置相关资产或负债时要求将相关利得或损失重分类为损益，主体应将与所有者权益减少相关的、之前确认为其他综合收益的相应的利得或损失重分类为损益。

权益法程序

26. 适合于权益法应用的许多程序与《国际财务报告准则第 10 号》中描述的合并程序类似。而且，对取得子公司进行会计处理所采用程序的基本概念，也在对取得联营企业或合营企业中投资进行会计处理时被采纳。

27. 集团在联营企业或合营企业中享有的份额是母公司及其子公司持有的该联营企业或合营企业的股份之和。集团其他联营企业或合营企业所持有的股份不予考虑。如果某一联营企业或合营企业拥有子公司、联营企业或合营企业，采用权益法时考虑的损益、其他综合收益以及净资产则是该联营企业或合营企业的财务报表中确认的部分（包括该联营企业或合营企业享有的其联营企业和合营企业的损益、其他综合收益以及净资产的份额），但是，在此之前为统一会计政策必须作相应调整（参见第 35 段和第 36 段）。

28. 主体（包括纳入合并财务报表范围的子公司）与联营企业或合营企业之间因“逆流”和“顺流”交易产生的利得和损失，在主体财务报表中确认的部分仅限于与非关联投资者在联营企业或合营企业中的权益相关的部分。“逆流”交易的例子，如将联营企业或合营企业的资产出售给投资者。“顺流”交易的例子，如将投资者的资产出售或赠予联营企业或合营企业。这些交易带来的投资者享有的联营企业或合营企业的损益份额应予抵销。

29. 当顺流交易表明出售或赠予的资产的可变现净值出现降低迹象或这些资产出现减值损失迹象，投资者应全额确认这些损失。当逆流交易表明购买资产的可变现净值出现降低迹象或这些资产出现减值损失迹象，投资者应确认其分担的损失份额。

30. 向联营企业或合营企业投入非货币性资产以换取联营企业或合营企业权益的，应当根据第 28 段进行会计处理，除非该投入缺乏如《国际会计准则第 16 号——不动产、厂场和设备》所定义的商业实质。如果该投入缺乏商业实质，相应的利得或损失被认为未实现，并不进行确认，除非第 31 段适用。该未实现利得和损失应从采用权益法进行会计处理的投资中予以剔除，不能在主体合并财务状况表或采用权益法对投资进行会计处理的主体财务状况表中作为递延利得或损失列报。

31. 如果主体除收到联营企业或合营企业的权益外，还收到货币性或非货币性资产，主体应将与货币性或非货币性资产相关的非货币性捐赠产生的利得或损失部分全额计入损益。

32. 对联营企业或合营企业的投资自其成为联营企业或合营企业之日起采用权益法进行会计处理。取得投资时，投资成本和主体享有的被投资者的可辨认资产和负债的公允价值净额份额之间的差额，按照下列方法进行会计处理：

（1）与联营企业或合营企业相关的商誉包括在投资的账面金额中。该商誉不允许摊销。

（2）主体享有的被投资者的可辨认资产和负债的公允价值净额份额超出投资成

本的部分，应在取得投资期间确定主体所享有的联营企业或合营企业的损益份额时包括在收益中。

例如，为基于取得投资日的公允价值对应计提折旧的资产的折旧进行会计处理，主体对取得投资后享有的联营企业或合营企业的损益也应当进行适当的调整。类似地，为反映诸如商誉或不动产、厂场和设备的减值损失，主体对取得投资后享有的联营企业或合营企业的损益应当进行适当的调整。

33. 应用权益法时，主体应使用联营企业或合营企业可获取的最近的财务报表。如果主体和联营企业或合营企业的报告期末日存在差异，为供主体使用，联营企业或合营企业应按照主体的财务报表日期编制财务报表，除非这样做不切实可行。

34. 根据第 33 段，当应用权益法时使用的联营企业或合营企业的财务报表的报告日期与主体的财务报表的报告日期存在差异时，应对联营企业或合营企业的财务报表报告日和主体财务报表报告日期之间所发生的重大交易或事项的影响进行调整。在任何情况下，联营企业或合营企业的报告日期和主体报告日期末日之间相差不得超过 3 个月。报告期长度以及报告期末日之间的差异在各期应相同。

35. 主体在编制其财务报表时，应对类似情况下相似交易和事项采用统一的会计政策。

36. 如果对类似情况下相似交易和事项，联营企业或合营企业采用的会计政策不同于主体，那么当主体在应用权益法使用联营企业或合营企业的财务报表时，应对其进行调整，以保证联营企业或合营企业的会计政策与主体会计政策一致。

37. 如果联营企业或合营企业有发行在外的累积优先股，并由主体以外的其他方持有且被归类为权益，主体应在对这些股份所分配的股利进行调整之后，才能计算所享有的损益份额，而不论股利是否已经宣告发放。

38. 如果主体享有的联营企业或合营企业的损失份额等于或超过主体在联营企业或合营企业中的权益，主体应停止确认其分担的未来损失份额。在联营企业或合营企业中的权益是权益法下对联营企业或合营企业投资的账面金额以及任何实质上构成主体对联营企业或合营企业的净投资的长期权益。例如，某一项目的清偿既没有计划，在可预见的未来期间也不可能进行，该项目实质上是主体在联营企业或合营企业中投资的延伸。这些项目可能包括优先股和长期应收款项或借款，但是不包括商业应收款项、商业应付款项或任何存在充分担保的长期应收款，例如担保贷款。权益法下确认的损失超过主体普通股投资的部分，按照优先级别（即清偿的优先权）逆序应用到主体在联营企业或合营企业权益中的其他部分。

39. 主体的权益降至零后，为额外的损失计提准备以及确认负债，仅限于主体发生的法定或推定义务，或代表联营企业或合营企业进行的支付。如果联营企业或合营企业之后报告了利润，只有在主体享有的利润份额等于未确认损失份额之后，主体才能恢复确认其享有的这些利润的份额。

减值损失

40. 采用权益法后，包括根据第38段确认联营企业或合营企业的损失后，主体应根据《国际会计准则第39号——金融工具：确认和计量》，确定是否有必要对主体在联营企业或合营企业中的净投资确认任何额外的减值损失。

41. 主体还应根据《国际会计准则第39号》，确定是否对不构成净投资的主体在联营企业或合营企业中的权益确认任何额外的减值损失，以及减值损失的金额。

42. 因为包括在对联营企业或合营企业投资的账面金额中的商誉并不是单独确认的，不须根据《国际会计准则第36号——资产减值》中关于商誉减值测试要求，对其进行单独的减值测试，而是根据《国际会计准则第36号》，通过比较投资的可收回金额（使用价值和公允价值减去出售费用后两者中的较高者）与账面金额，将投资的整体账面金额作为一项资产进行减值测试，无论抵销《国际会计准则第39号》是否表明投资可能发生减值。在这种情况下确认的减值损失不分配给包括商誉在内的构成联营企业或合营企业投资账面金额的任何资产。相应地，按照《国际会计准则第36号》确认的减值损失的转回金额仅限于投资在后续增加的可回收金额。为了确定投资的使用价值，主体应估计：

（1）联营企业或合营企业预期将产生的预计未来现金流量的现值中主体享有的份额，包括联营企业或合营企业的经营活动带来的现金流量以及最终处置投资的　；或者

（2）从投资中收取的股利以及从最终对投资的处置中可望产生的预计未来现金流量的现值。

在恰当的假设下，两种方法将得出相同的结果。

43. 在联营企业或合营企业中投资的可收回金额，将按单个联营企业或合营企业进行评估，除非某一联营企业或合营企业在持续使用中无法产生独立于主体其他资产的现金流入。

单独财务报表

44. 在主体的单独财务报表中，在联营企业或合营企业中的投资应当根据《国际会计准则第27号》（2011年修改）第10段的规定进行处理。

生效日期和过渡性规定

45. 主体应当自2013年1月1日或以后开始的年度期间采用本准则。允许提前采

用。如果主体提前采用本准则，应披露这一事实，并同时采用《国际财务报告准则第 10 号》、《国际财务报告准则第 11 号——合营安排》、《国际财务报告准则第 12 号——在其他主体中权益的披露》和《国际会计准则第 27 号》（2011 年修改）。

参照《国际财务报告准则第 9 号》

46. 如果主体采用了本准则，但尚未采用《国际财务报告准则第 9 号》，对《国际财务报告准则第 9 号》的参照应理解为对《国际会计准则第 39 号》的参照。

《国际会计准则第 28 号》（2003）的撤销

47. 本准则取代了《国际会计准则第 28 号——联营中的投资》（2003 年修订）。

理事会批准 2003 年 12 月发布的《国际会计准则第 28 号》

国际会计准则理事会 14 位理事会同意批准发布《国际会计准则第 28 号——联营中的投资》。

David Tweedie 爵士	主席
Thomas E Jones	副主席
Mary E Barth	
Hans Georg Bruns	
Anthony T Cope	
Robert P Garnett	
Gilbert Gélard	
James J Leisenring	
Warren J McGregor	
Patricia L O'Malley	
Harry K Schmid	
John T Smith	
Geoffrey Whittington	
Tatsumi Yamada	

《国际会计准则第 28 号——在联营企业和合营企业中的投资》结论基础

本结论基础与《国际会计准则第 28 号》一并发布，但不构成其组成部分。

引言

1. 本结论基础概述了国际会计准则理事会在 2011 年修改《国际会计准则第 28 号——联营企业中的投资》形成结论过程中所考虑的因素。理事会理事个人对有些因素比对其他因素更为重视。

2. 《国际会计准则第 28 号》的修改源于理事会的合营企业项目。在考虑合营企业项目时，理事会决定将合营企业的会计处理并入《国际会计准则第 28 号》，因为权益法适用于合营企业和联营企业。

3. 因此，《国际会计准则第 28 号》的名称改为《在联营企业和合营企业中的投资》。由于理事会的本意不是重新考虑《国际会计准则第 28 号》中有关对联营企业中投资的会计处理的基本方法，理事会将未重新考虑的《国际会计准则第 28 号》（2003 年修订）中的结论基础并入《国际会计准则第 28 号》的结论基础中。

《国际会计准则第 28 号》的结构和理事会的考虑

4. 2011 年修改的《国际会计准则第 28 号》取代了 2003 年修订、2010 年修改的《国际会计准则第 28 号》。正如第 3 段所述，在修改《国际会计准则第 28 号》过程中，理事会没有重新考虑本准则的所有规定。第 5 段至 11 段、第 15 段、第 22 段至 23 段、第 25 段至 28 段以及第 32 段至 43 段中的规定与重大影响的评估、权益法及其应用相关，第 12 段至 14 段与潜在表决权的会计处理相关。除理事会决定将合营企业会计处理并入《国际会计准则第 28 号》外，这些段落都来自《国际会计准则第 28 号》，以及《国际会计准则第 27 号——合并财务报表和单独财务报表》、《国际会计准则第28号——联营中的投资》、《国际会计准则第31号——合营企业中的权益》的应用指南，这些指南在《国际财务报告准则第10号——合并财务报表》、《国际财务报告准则第11号——合营安排》和《国际会计准则第28号》（2011年修改）发布时予以撤销。因此，那些段落未被理事会重新考虑。

5. 在2003年修订时，结论基础与《国际会计准则第28号》一并发布，概述了理事会在形成当时结论过程中所考虑的因素。该结论基础后续作了更新，以反映对本准则的修改。

6. 理事会将原先结论基础的内容并入了《国际会计准则第28号》（2011年修改）的结论基础，因为原先的结论基础涉及了理事会未重新考虑的问题。这些内容的段落号以“Z”作为前缀加以标识。在这些段落中，交叉索引之处已经对应作了更新，文字上也作了必要的细微改动。

7. 一位理事不同意2008年5月发布的对《国际会计准则第28号》所做的修改，这些修改已经列入《国际会计准则第28号》（2011年修改）。他的不同意见也在本结论基础后列出。

8. 第2段、第16段至21段、第24段和第29段至31段的规定与合营企业项目中解决的问题相关，这导致对《国际会计准则第28号》进行修改。

9. 作为合并财务报表项目的一部分，理事会正在检查投资主体如何对其在子公司、合营企业和联营企业中的权益进行会计处理。其结论可能影响到风险资本组织、共同基金、信托公司和类似主体对在联营企业和合营企业中的权益进行会计处理的方法。理事会期望在2011年晚些时候发布关于投资主体的征求意见稿。

范围

10. 在重新考虑《征求意见稿第9号——合营安排》过程中，理事会重新考虑了《国际会计准则第31号》中有关范围排除的规定，《征求意见稿第9号》也有这方面的建议。理事会得出结论，按照《国际财务报告准则第9号——金融工具》以公允价值计量且其变动计入损益的风险资本组织、共同基金、信托公司和包括投连险基金在内的类似主体持有的合营企业中的权益被排除在《征求意见稿第9号》范围之外，该内容更适合作为计量豁免，而不是作为范围排除。

11. 理事会观察到，风险资本组织、共同基金、信托公司和包括投连险基金在内的类似主体持有的联营企业中的权益按照《国际财务报告准则第9号》以公允价值计量且其变动计入损益时，也被类似地排除在《国际会计准则第28号》范围之外。

12. 理事会观察到，《征求意见稿第9号》和《国际会计准则第28号》中作出的范围排除，不是因为这些安排不具有合营安排的特征或者这些投资不属于联营企业，而是因为对于风险资本组织、共同基金、信托公司和包括投连险基金在内的类似主体持有的投资，公允价值计量向财务报表使用者提供了比应用权益法更有用的信息。

13. 因此，理事会决定保留允许风险资本组织、共同基金、信托公司和包括投连险基金在内的类似主体按照《国际财务报告准则第 9 号》对在合营和联营企业中的权益以公允价值计量且其变动计入损益的选择权，但明确这是采用权益法计量联营企业和合营企业中权益规定的豁免，而不是《国际会计准则第 28 号》关于这些主体持有的联营企业和合营企业投资的会计处理的范围排除。

14. 基于上述决定和将合营企业会计处理并入《国际会计准则第 28 号》的决定，理事会决定《国际会计准则第 28 号》应适用于对被投资者具有共同控制或重大影响的所有主体持有投资的会计处理。

重大影响

潜在表决权

15. 在考虑修改《国际会计准则第 28 号》时，为了与合并报表项目的规定保持一致，理事会考虑了目前《国际会计准则第 28 号》第 7 段至 9 段关于评估重大影响时有关潜在表决权的规定是否应做变动。

16. 理事会观察到，《国际会计准则第 28 号》中重大影响的定义（即参与被投资者的财务和经营政策决策的权力，但不是控制或共同控制这些政策）与《国际会计准则第 27 号》中的控制定义相关。理事会在修改《国际会计准则第 28 号》时还没有考虑重大影响的定义，并作出决定，单独改变重大影响的一个要素是不恰当的。任何此类考虑都应当在更广范围内审议对联营企业的会计处理时作为其中一部分进行。

权益法的应用

暂时的共同控制和重大影响（2003 年修订）

Z17. 在《国际财务报告准则第 5 号——持有待售的非流动资产和终止经营》中，理事会决定当对被投资者的共同控制或重大影响意图为暂时性的情况下不豁免主体应用权益法对联营企业和合营企业中的投资进行会计处理。

削弱向投资者转移资金能力的严格的长期性限制（2003 年修订）

Z18. 理事会决定，当严格的长期性限制削弱了联营企业或合营企业向投资者转移资金的能力时，不豁免主体应用权益法对联营企业和合营企业中的投资进行会计处理。理事会这样决定是因为这种情况可能并不会妨碍主体对联营企业或合营企业的共同控制或重大影响。理事会认为，主体在评价其对被投资者实施共同控制或重大影响的能力时，应当考虑该联营企业或合营企业向主体转移资金时存在的限制。但这些限制本身并不妨碍共同控制或重大影响的存在。

年末时点不一致（2003 年修订）

Z19.《国际会计准则第 28 号》2003 年修订前的征求意见稿建议，应用权益法时，主体与联营企业或合营企业的报告日相差应限制在三个月以内。一些征求意见稿的反馈意见者认为，如果主体与联营企业或合营企业的财务报告日相差超过三个月，那么要求主体编制同一日的财务报表不具有可行性。理事会注意到，三个月的限制在一些国家或地区已经使用，而如果放宽时间，比如六个月，则会导致确认过时的信息。因此，理事会决定维持三个月的限制。

豁免应用权益法：联营企业中部分投资使用公允价值计量

20. 理事会收到一份请求，要求明确在联营企业中的部分投资按照《国际会计准则第 28 号》第 18 段的规定没有采用权益法进行会计处理，而是按照《国际财务报告准则第 9 号》以公允价值计量且其变动计入损益的情况下，该联营企业中投资的不同部分是否可以采用不同的计量基础。理事会最初考虑将《国际会计准则第 28 号》的修改作为 2010 年 4 月发布的《国际财务报告准则的改进》的一部分，然而在 2010 年 2 月的会议上，理事会决定在合营企业项目中解决这个问题。

21. 理事会注意到，关于计量存在两种观点。第一种观点确认母公司自己或通过其任一子公司直接或间接持有联营企业的权益，然后对在联营企业中的全部投资适用《国际会计准则第 28 号》。根据这种观点，联营企业中仅有一项投资，应当作为一个单元进行会计处理。第二种观点确认在联营企业中直接或间接持有的权益，但是，如果联营企业中的部分投资被风险资本组织、共同基金、信托公司和包括投连险基金在内的类似主体持有，不管这些主体对联营企业中的部分投资是否具有重大影响，都允许对这部分投资使用计量豁免。理事会同意第二种观点，因此决定修改《国际会计准则第 28 号》。理事会决定对合营企业中的部分投资使用公允价值计量不提供相应的指南，因为理事会认为这样的事项在实务中不大可能发生。

22. 理事会也讨论了是否仅当风险资本组织、共同基金、信托公司和包括投连险基金在内的类似主体已经在其自身财务报表中，将其在联营企业中的这部分投资指定为以公允价值计量且其变动计入损益时，才允许部分投资使用公允价值。理事会注意到，可能出现主体对其在联营企业中的投资没有采用以公允价值计量且其变动计入损益的一些情况。然而在这些情况中，从集团的角度来看，对商业目的的恰当判断将导致在合并财务报表中对其在联营企业中的这部分投资以公允价值计量且其变动计入损益。因此，理事会决定，主体应当能够对风险资本组织、共同基金、信托公司和包括投连险基金在内的类似主体持有的在联营企业中部分投资以公允价值计量且其变动计入损益，而不管这部分投资在这些主体财务报表上是否以公允价值计量且其变动计入损益。

分类为持有待售

23. 《征求意见稿第9号》建议，主体应按照《国际财务报告准则第5号》对被分类为持有待售的在合营企业中的权益进行会计处理。

24. 理事会在对《征求意见稿第9号》重新考虑的过程中注意到，2009年8月发布的《国际财务报告准则的改进》征求意见稿建议修改《国际财务报告准则第5号》，要求主体在导致丧失重大影响或共同控制的出售计划中负有承诺时，将在联营企业或共同控制主体中的权益分类为持有待售。这些建议旨在明确主体在导致对该权益丧失重大影响或共同控制的出售计划中负有承诺时，必须将其在联营企业或合营企业中的所有权益（“整个权益”）分类为持有待售。

25. 理事会发现，这些建议与理事会在重新考虑《征求意见稿第9号》时所做的决定不一致。该决定删除了将丧失共同控制和重大影响与“重要经济事项”术语联系在一起的所有表述，该术语是理事会在企业合并项目第二阶段中引入的（参见结论基础第28段至31段）。

26. 理事会决定，将权益分类为持有待售应当基于计划的处置方案是否符合《国际财务报告准则第5号》中分类为持有待售的标准，而不是基于主体是否已经丧失对权益的共同控制或重大影响。因此，理事会得出结论，当主体对联营企业或合营企业中的权益或部分权益的处置符合《国际财务报告准则第5号》中分类为持有待售的标准时，主体应将整个权益或部分权益分类为持有待售。

27. 理事会决定，在部分处置的情况下，主体应对联营企业或合营企业中的剩余权益继续使用权益法，直到分类为持有待售的权益部分最终被处置完。理事会对此的解释是，即使主体有意图出售联营企业或合营企业中的部分权益，在出售前，主体仍对被投资者具有重大影响或共同控制。处置后，主体应按照《国际财务报告准则第9号》对合营或联营企业中的剩余权益进行会计处理，如果主体对剩余权益仍具有重大影响或共同控制则按照《国际会计准则第28号》进行会计处理。

终止采用权益法

28. 理事会在重新考虑《征求意见稿第9号》的过程中，重新考虑了在企业合并项目第二阶段中将丧失共同控制或重大影响作为重要经济事项（正如将丧失控制作为重要经济事项那样）的决定是否合适。如果合适，理事会认为，应要求主体按照《国际财务报告准则第10号》的规定重新校准相应会计处理。然而，理事会作出决定，尽管这些事项很重要，但本质上是不同的。在丧失控制的情况下，母子公司关系的终止导致资产和负债的终止确认，因为集团的组织结构发生了变化。如果丧失共同控制或重大影响，集团的组织结构不会受到影响。

29. 理事会还注意到，当剩余权益是一项金融资产时在丧失共同控制或重大影响的情况下保留重要经济事项的特征是没有必要的。《国际财务报告准则第9号》已经要求在这些情况下剩余权益（即金融资产）必须以公允价值计量。

30. 在丧失共同控制但仍具有重大影响的情况下，理事会承认投资者与被投资者的关系发生了变化，因此投资的性质也发生了变化。然而，在这种情况下，这两种投资（即合营企业和联营企业）继续采用权益法计量。考虑到集团边界没有发生变化，计量要求也没有发生变化，理事会得出结论，丧失共同控制但仍具有重大影响并不是导致对剩余权益以公允价值重新计量的事项。

31. 因此，理事会删除了企业合并项目第二阶段中引入的将失去共同控制或重大影响作为重要经济事项的所有描述。

并入《解释公告第13号》

32. 在合营企业项目中，理事会决定将《国际会计准则第28号》中对主体与联营企业之间"顺流"和"逆流"交易会计处理的规定和指南扩展至主体与合营企业之间"顺流"和"逆流"交易的会计处理。

33. 在《征求意见稿第9号》中，理事会建议将《解释公告第13号——共同控制主体：合营者的非货币性投入》中的一致意见并入合营安排准则。因为理事会将所有关于合营企业的会计处理规定重新放入《国际会计准则第28号》，理事会将《解释公告第13号》中的一致意见并入《国际会计准则第28号》，并将其扩展至联营企业。

34. 理事会注意到，除下列方面，《解释公告第13号》中关于合营者[①]对合营企业的非货币性投入的一致意见与《国际会计准则第28号》相符。《解释公告第13号》在确认归属于其他方权益的利得或损失时设定了三种例外情况。在回应《征求意见稿第9号》反馈意见时，理事会重新考虑将《解释公告第13号》包括的例外并入《国际会计准则第28号》的需要，该例外涉及主体对归属于其他非关联投资者在被投资者中权益的部分利得和损失的确认。

35. 理事会得出结论，只有当交易缺乏商业实质时才将《解释公告第13号》一致意见中确认利得或损失的例外引入《国际会计准则第28号》，因为《解释公告第13号》中的其他两种例外（即"与投入的非货币性资产所有权有关的重大风险和报酬没有转移给共同控制主体"和"非货币性投入的利得和损失不能可靠地计量"）或者不符合《国际财务报告准则第11号》的原则和规定，或者与已经包括在《财务报

① 2011年5月发布的《国际财务报告准则第11号——合营安排》使用术语"合营者"表示对合营企业拥有共同控制的参与方。

告概念框架》中利得或损失的确认标准（即“计量的可靠性”）相关。

Z36. 对于主体在一定程度上，收到的、与被投资者中股东权益以外的投入资产不相类似的货币性或非货币性资产，其实现不取决于被投资者未来的现金流量，盈利过程已经完成。因此，主体应在损益中全部确认与收到的货币性或非货币性资产相关的非货币性投入的利得或损失部分。

37. 此外，理事会考虑了《国际会计准则第 31 号》关于顺流或逆流交易表明交易或投入的资产的可变现净值减少或发生减值损失时损失的确认规定是否相关，并决定将这些规定并入《国际会计准则第 28 号》。

损失的确认（2003 年修订）

Z38. 2000 年版的《国际会计准则第 28 号》和《解释公告第 20 号——权益法：损失的确认》规定，在核算主体的损失份额中，当投资的账面金额减记至零时，限制采用权益法。

Z39. 理事会决定，可减记至零的基数应不限于剩余所有者权益性利益，还应当包括本质上是对联营企业或合营企业净投资一部分的其他非所有者权益性利益，如长期应收款。因此，理事会决定撤销《解释公告第 20 号》。

Z40. 理事会还注意到，如果可减记至零的基数不包括非权益性投资，则主体可能对其投资进行重组，将大部分投资转为非权益性投资，以避免在权益法下确认来自联营企业或合营企业的损失。

Z41. 在扩展损失确认的基数时，理事会也明确了《国际会计准则第 39 号——金融工具：确认和计量》的减值规定对构成净投资一部分的金融资产的适用性。

减值损失（2008 年修改）

Z42. 2008 年，理事会发现《国际会计准则第 28 号》中一项较含糊的指南，是关于减值转回在多大程度上应确认为在联营企业或合营企业中投资的账面金额的调整。

Z43. 理事会注意到，应用权益法涉及调整主体对联营企业或合营企业诸如商誉、不动产、厂场和设备等资产上确认的减值损失份额，以考虑这些资产取得日的公允价值。理事会在 2007 年 10 月发布的征求意见稿《国际财务报告准则的改进》中建议，主体采用权益法后新确认的额外减值不应分配到构成该投资账面金额一部分的任何资产上，包括商誉。因此，这样的减值应在以后期间在投资的可收回金额增加的范围内转回。

Z44. 征求意见稿的一些意见反馈者表示，建议的修改与《国际会计准则第 39 号》（关于可供出售权益工具减值损失的转回）或者《国际会计准则第 36 号——资产减值》（关于商誉减值损失的分配和与商誉相关的减值损失的任何转回）不一致。

Z45. 理事会在重新考虑过程中重申了以前的决定，但为回应提出的反馈意见，理事会决定澄清修订的原因。理事会决定，主体不应将减值损失分配到联营企业或合营企业中投资账面金额一部分的任何资产，因为该投资是主体控制并确认的唯一资产。

Z46. 理事会还决定，减值损失的任何转回应在该投资的可收回金额增加的范围内确认为对联营企业或合营中投资的调整。该规定与《国际会计准则第 36 号》一致，该准则允许转回除商誉以外的资产的减值损失。理事会不认为该减值损失转回的规定应与《国际会计准则第 39 号》中关于权益工具或值损失转回的规定保持一致，因为主体根据《国际会计准则第 36 号》而不是根据《国际会计准则第 39 号》确认对联营企业或合营企业投资的减值损失。

生效日期和过渡性规定

47. 理事会决定将本准则的生效日期与《国际财务报告准则第 10 号》、《国际财务报告准则第 11 号》、《国际财务报告准则第 12 号——在其他主体中权益的披露》、《国际会计准则第 27 号——单独财务报表》的生效日期保持一致。当作出该决定时，理事会注意到这五项国际财务报告准则都与报告主体与其他主体间特殊关系（即报告主体对其他主体具有控制、共同控制或重大影响）的评估、相关会计处理以及披露规定有关。因此，理事会得出结论，应用《国际会计准则第 28 号》而不应用其他四项国际财务报告准则可能引起不必要的混乱。

48. 理事会通常将生效日期定为国际财务报告准则发布后 12 个月至 18 个月之间。在考虑这些国际财务报告准则的生效日期时，理事会考虑了以下因素：

（1）许多国家要求的翻译时间和将强制性规定引入法律的时间。

（2）合并财务报表项目与始于 2007 年爆发的全球金融危机有关，为响应二十国集团领导人、金融稳定理事会、财务报表使用者、监管机构和其他方有关改善主体“资产负债表外”活动的会计处理和披露的迫切要求，理事会加快了相应的步伐。

（3）收到的关于 2010 年 10 月发布的《意见征询——生效日期和过渡性规定》的反馈意见，该《意见征询》是关于 2011 年发布的国际财务报告准则的执行成本、生效日期和过渡性规定。大多数反馈意见者并不认为合并报表和合营安排国际财务报告准则会严重影响执行这些准则所需要的时间和资源。此外，只有少数意见反馈者认为这些国际财务报告准则的生效日期应与 2011 年发布的其他国际财务报告准则的生效日期保持一致。

49. 考虑这些因素后，理事会决定要求主体在 2013 年 1 月 1 日或以后日期开始的年度期间采用这五项国际财务报告准则。

50. 该《意见征询》的大多数反馈意见者支持提前采用 2011 年发布的国际财务报告准则。意见反馈者强调，提前采用对 2011 年和 2012 年首次采用国际财务报告准则的主体尤其重要。理事会被这些意见说服，决定允许提前采用《国际会计准则第 28 号》，但主体必须和其他国际财务报告准则［即《国际财务报告准则第 10 号》、《国际财务报告准则第 11 号》、《国际财务报告准则第 12 号》和《国际会计准则第 27 号》（2011 年修改）］一并提前采用，以避免财务报表之间缺乏可比性，鉴于结论基础第 47 段提出的原因，理事会决定为这五项国际财务报告准则设定同一个生效日期。尽管主体应同时采用这五项国际财务报告准则，理事会注意到，如果按照《国际财务报告准则第 12 号》提前提供信息能使使用者更好地理解主体与其他主体间的关系，则不应阻止主体提前提供《国际财务报告准则第 12 号》所要求的信息。

概述

撤销《国际会计准则第 28 号》（2003 年修订）

51. 《国际会计准则第 28 号——在联营企业和合营企业中的投资》取代了《国际会计准则第 28 号——联营中的投资》（2003 年修订，2010 年修改）。《国际会计准则第 28 号》（2011 年修改）并入了合营企业的会计处理和理事会在重新考虑《征求意见稿第 9 号》过程中讨论的一些修改。

披露

52. 《国际会计准则第 28 号》没有涉及对被投资者具有共同控制或重大影响的主体的披露要求。作为对《征求意见稿第 9 号》和《征求意见稿第 10 号——合并财务报表》重新考虑的一部分，理事会发现了一个可以将子公司、合营安排、联营企业以及未纳入合并财务报表范围的结构化主体的披露要求整合到一起并保持一致的机会，将这些要求并入单个国际财务报告准则中。

53. 理事会观察到，《国际会计准则第 27 号》、《国际会计准则第 28 号》和《国际会计准则第 31 号》包含许多相似的披露要求。《征求意见稿第 9 号》已经建议对联营企业和合营企业的披露要求进行修改，使这两类投资的披露要求更加相近。理事会注意到，大多数意见反馈者同意《征求意见稿第 9 号》的建议，使合营企业的披露要求与《国际会计准则第 28 号》中对联营企业的披露要求保持一致。

54. 因此，理事会将在子公司、合营安排、联营企业以及非纳入合并财务报表结构化主体中的权益的披露要求整合到单个综合准则中，即《国际财务报告准则第 12 号》。

55. 与《国际财务报告准则第 12 号》一并发布的结论基础总结了理事会制定该国际财务报告准则的考虑，包括对《征求意见稿第 9 号》披露建议的反馈意见的审议。因此，《国际会计准则第 28 号》没有包括披露要求，本结论基础也没有包括理事会对《征求意见稿第 9 号》建议的披露要求反馈意见的考虑。

对《国际会计准则第 28 号》（2003 年修订）的主要变动概述

56. 对《国际会计准则第 28 号》以前版本的主要变动如下：

（1）合营企业的会计处理被并入本准则。

（2）删除了针对风险资本组织、共同基金、信托公司和包括投连险基金在内的类似主体的范围排除，将其作为在联营企业和合营企业中的投资使用权益法计量的计量豁免。

（3）《国际会计准则第 28 号》现在允许在联营企业中拥有投资，且通过风险资本组织、共同基金、信托公司和包括投连险基金在内的类似主体间接持有部分投资的主体按照《国际财务报告准则第 9 号》对联营企业中这部分投资选择以公允价值计量且其变动计入损益，不管这些主体对该部分投资是否具有重大影响。

（4）《国际会计准则第 28 号》要求在联营企业或合营企业中的部分投资分类为持有待售，如果这部分权益的处置符合《国际财务报告准则第 5 号》中关于分类为持有待售的标准。

（5）《解释公告第 13 号》的一致意见已并入《国际会计准则第 28 号》。因此，为交换联营企业或合营企业中所有者权益而对联营企业或合营企业投入的非货币性资产所产生的利得和损失仅在联营企业或合营企业的非关联投资者权益范围内予以确认，除非该投入缺乏如《国际会计准则第 16 号——不动产、厂场和设备》中定义的商业实质。

（6）披露要求由《国际财务报告准则第 12 号》规范。

不同意见

对 2008 年 5 月发布的修改的不同意见

山田辰己的不同意见

1. 山田先生投票反对 2008 年 5 月发布的《国际财务报告准则的改进》中关于《国际会计准则第 28 号——联营中的投资》的一处修改。

2. 山田先生认为不将新增的减值损失分配至商誉和构成联营企业投资账面金额的其他资产是不恰当的。在他看来，因为他认为投资者在作出投资决策时能够辨认可归属的商誉，投资者确认的在联营企业中的投资的减值损失应当分配至商誉和构成联营企业投资账面金额的其他资产。

3. 山田先生还认为被分配到商誉中的所有减值损失不应在后期转回。在他看来，正如该修改规定的，未分配至商誉的减值损失和后期转回的减值损失实质上导致确认了内部产生的商誉。他认为，《国际会计准则第 28 号》的修改与《国际会计准则第 36 号——资产减值》第 124 段和 125 段不符，这两段禁止与商誉相关的减值损失转回。

对照表

本表显示了被取代的《国际会计准则第 28 号》（2003 年修订）版本与 2011 年修改的《国际会计准则第 28 号》版本内容的对应关系。尽管被取代的《国际会计准则第 28 号》版本中的一些规定已并入《国际财务报告准则第 12 号——在其他主体中权益的披露》，本表还是显示这些段落的对应关系。即便相应的指南不同，但如果这些段落大体规范了相同的事项，它们也视为可以相互对应。

被取代的《国际会计准则第 28 号》段落	修改的《国际会计准则第 28 号》段落	《国际财务报告准则第 12 号》段落	修改的《国际会计准则第 27 号》段落
1	2，18，19		
2	3，4		
3			7
4			6
5			8
6	5		
7	6		
8	7		
9	8		
10	9		
11	10		
12	12		
13	17		
14	20		
15	21		
17	11		
18	22		
19	22		
19A	23		
20	26		
21	27		
22	28		
23	32		
24	33		

续表

被取代的《国际会计准则第28号》段落	修改的《国际会计准则第28号》段落	《国际财务报告准则第12号》段落	修改的《国际会计准则第27号》段落
25	34		
26	35		
27	36		
28	37		
29	38		
30	39		
31	40		
32	41		
33	42		
34	43		
35	44		
36			3
37		21－24	
38		21－24	
39		21－24	
40		21－24	
41	45		
41A－41E			
42	47		
43	47		
无	1，13－16，24，25，29－31，46		

International Accounting Standard 28
Investments in Associates and Joint Ventures

CONTENTS

INTRODUCTION	IN1 – IN11
INTERNATIONAL ACCOUNTING STANDARD 28 INVESTMENTS IN ASSOCIATES AND JOINT VENTURES	
OBJECTIVE	1
SCOPE	2
DEFINITIONS	3 – 4
SIGNIFICANT INFLUENCE	5 – 9
EQUITY METHOD	10 – 15
APPLICATION OF THE EQUITY METHOD	16 – 43
Exemptions from applying the equity method	17 – 19
Classification as held for sale	20 – 21
Discontinuing the use of the equity method	22 – 24
Changes in ownership interest	25
Equity method procedures	26 – 39
Impairment losses	40 – 43
SEPARATE FINANCIAL STATEMENTS	44
EFFECTIVE DATE AND TRANSITION	45 – 46
References to IFRS 9	46
WITHDRAWAL OF IAS 28 (2003)	47
APPROVAL BY THE BOARD OF IAS 28 ISSUED IN DECEMBER 2003	
Basis for Conclusions on IAS 28 Investments in Associates and Joint Ventures	
DISSENTING OPINION	
TABLE OF CONCORDANCE	

International Accounting Standard 28 *Investments in Associates and Joint Ventures* (IAS 28) is set out in paragraphs 1 – 47. All the paragraphs have equal authority but retain the IASC format of the Standard when it was adopted by the IASB. IAS 28 should be read in the context of its objective and the Basis for Conclusions, the *Preface to International Financial Reporting Standards* and the *Conceptual Framework for Financial Reporting*. IAS 8 *Accounting Policies, Changes in Accounting Estimates and Errors* provides a basis for selecting and applying accounting policies in the absence of explicit guidance.

Introduction

IN1 International Accounting Standard 28 *Investments in Associates and Joint Ventures* (IAS 28) prescribes the accounting for investments in associates and sets out the requirements for the application of the equity method when accounting for investments in associates and joint ventures.

IN2 The Standard is effective for annual periods beginning on or after 1 January 2013. Earlier application is permitted.

Main features of the Standard

IN3 IAS 28 (as amended in 2011) is to be applied by all entities that are investors with joint control of, or significant influence over, an investee.

IN4 The Standard defines significant influence as the power to participate in the financial and operating policy decisions of the investee but is not control or joint control of those policies.

IN5 IFRS 11 *Joint Arrangements* establishes principles for the financial reporting of parties to joint arrangements. It defines joint control as the contractually agreed sharing of control of an arrangement, which exists only when decisions about the relevant activities require the unanimous consent of the parties sharing control.

IN6 An entity applies IFRS 11 to determine the type of joint arrangement in which it is involved. Once it has determined that it has an interest in a joint venture, the entity recognises an investment and accounts for it using the equity method in accordance with IAS 28 (as amended in 2011), unless the entity is exempted from applying the equity method as specified in the Standard.

Equity method

IN7 The Standard defines the equity method as a method of accounting whereby the investment is initially recognised at cost and adjusted thereafter for the post-acquisition change in the investor's share of net assets of the investee. The profit or loss of the investor includes its share of the profit or loss of the investee and the other comprehensive income of the investor includes its share of other comprehensive income of the investee.

IN8 An entity uses the equity method to account for its investments in associates or joint ventures in its consolidated financial statements. An entity that does not have any subsidiaries also uses the equity method to account for its investments in associates or joint ventures in its financial statements even though those are not described as consolidated financial statements. The only financial statements to which an entity does not apply the equity method are separate financial statements it presents in accordance with IAS 27 *Separate Financial Statements* .

Exemptions from applying the equity method

IN9 The Standard provides exemptions from applying the equity method similar to those provided in IFRS 10 *Consolidated Financial Statements* for parents not to prepare consolidated financial statements.

IN10 The Standard also provides exemptions from applying the equity method when the investment in the associate or joint venture is held by, or is held indirectly through, venture capital organisations, or mutual funds, unit trusts and similar entities including investment-linked insurance funds. Those investments in associates and joint ventures may be measured at fair value through profit or loss in accordance with IFRS 9 *Financial Instruments*.

Disclosure

IN11 The disclosure requirements for entities with joint control of, or significant influence over, an investee are specified in IFRS 12 *Disclosure of Interests in Other Entities* .

International Accounting Standard 28
Investments in Associates and Joint Ventures

Objective

1 **The objective of this Standard is to prescribe the accounting for investments in associates and to set out the requirements for the application of the equity method when accounting for investments in associates and joint ventures.**

Scope

2 **This Standard shall be applied by all entities that are investors with joint control of, or significant influence over, an investee.**

Definitions

3 **The following terms are used in this Standard with the meanings specified:**

An *associate* is an entity over which the investor has significant influence.

***Consolidated financial statements* are the financial statements of a group in which assets, liabilities, equity, income, expenses and cash flows of the parent and its subsidiaries are presented as those of a single economic entity.**

The *equity method* is a method of accounting whereby the investment is initially recognised at cost and adjusted thereafter for the post-acquisition change in the investor's share of the investee's net assets. The investor's profit or loss includes its share of the investee's profit or loss and the investor's other comprehensive income includes its share of the investee's other comprehensive income.

A *joint arrangement* is an arrangement of which two or more parties have joint control.

***Joint control* is the contractually agreed sharing of control of an arrangement, which exists only when decisions about the relevant activities require the unanimous consent of the parties sharing control.**

A *joint venture* is a joint arrangement whereby the parties that have joint control of the arrangement have rights to the net assets of the arrangement.

A *joint venturer* is a party to a joint venture that has joint control of that joint

venture.

Significant influence **is the power to participate in the financial and operating policy decisions of the investee but is not control or joint control of those policies.**

4 The following terms are defined in paragraph 4 of IAS 27 *Separate Financial Statements* and in Appendix A of IFRS 10 *Consolidated Financial Statements* and are used in this Standard with the meanings specified in the IFRSs in which they are defined:

- control of an investee
- group
- parent
- separate financial statements
- subsidiary.

Significant influence

5 If an entity holds, directly or indirectly (eg through subsidiaries), 20 per cent or more of the voting power of the investee, it is presumed that the entity has significant influence, unless it can be clearly demonstrated that this is not the case. Conversely, if the entity holds, directly or indirectly (eg through subsidiaries), less than 20 per cent of the voting power of the investee, it is presumed that the entity does not have significant influence, unless such influence can be clearly demonstrated. A substantial or majority ownership by another investor does not necessarily preclude an entity from having significant influence.

6 The existence of significant influence by an entity is usually evidenced in one or more of the following ways:

(a) representation on the board of directors or equivalent governing body of the investee;

(b) participation in policy-making processes, including participation in decisions about dividends or other distributions;

(c) material transactions between the entity and its investee;

(d) interchange of managerial personnel; or

(e) provision of essential technical information.

7 An entity may own share warrants, share call options, debt or equity instruments that are convertible into ordinary shares, or other similar instruments that have the potential, if exercised or converted, to give the entity additional voting power or to reduce another party's voting power over the financial and operating policies of another entity (ie potential voting rights). The existence and effect of potential voting rights that are currently exercisable or convertible, including potential voting rights held by other entities, are considered when assessing whether an entity has significant influence. Potential voting rights are not currently exercisable or convertible when, for example, they cannot be exercised or converted until a future date or until the occurrence of a future event.

8 In assessing whether potential voting rights contribute to significant influence, the entity examines all facts and circumstances (including the terms of exercise of the potential voting rights and any other contractual arrangements whether considered individually or in combination) that affect potential rights, except the intentions of management and the financial ability to exercise or convert those potential rights.

9 An entity loses significant influence over an investee when it loses the power to participate in the financial and operating policy decisions of that investee. The loss of significant influence can occur with or without a change in absolute or relative ownership levels. It could occur, for example, when an associate becomes subject to the control of a government, court, administrator or regulator. It could also occur as a result of a contractual arrangement.

Equity method

10 Under the equity method, on initial recognition the investment in an associate or a joint venture is recognised at cost, and the carrying amount is increased or decreased to recognise the investor's share of the profit or loss of the investee after the date of acquisition. The investor's share of the investee's profit or loss is recognised in the investor's profit or loss. Distributions received from an investee reduce the carrying amount of the investment. Adjustments to the carrying amount may also be necessary for changes in the investor's proportionate interest in the investee arising from changes in the investee's other comprehensive income. Such changes include those arising from the revaluation of property, plant and equipment and from foreign exchange translation differences. The investor's share of those changes is recognised in the investor's other comprehensive income (see IAS 1 *Presentation of Financial Statements*).

11 The recognition of income on the basis of distributions received may not be an adequate

measure of the income earned by an investor on an investment in an associate or a joint venture because the distributions received may bear little relation to the performance of the associate or joint venture. Because the investor has joint control of, or significant influence over, the investee, the investor has an interest in the associate's or joint venture's performance and, as a result, the return on its investment. The investor accounts for this interest by extending the scope of its financial statements to include its share of the profit or loss of such an investee. As a result, application of the equity method provides more informative reporting of the investor's net assets and profit or loss.

12 When potential voting rights or other derivatives containing potential voting rights exist, an entity's interest in an associate or a joint venture is determined solely on the basis of existing ownership interests and does not reflect the possible exercise or conversion of potential voting rights and other derivative instruments, unless paragraph 13 applies.

13 In some circumstances, an entity has, in substance, an existing ownership as a result of a transaction that currently gives it access to the returns associated with an ownership interest. In such circumstances, the proportion allocated to the entity is determined by taking into account the eventual exercise of those potential voting rights and other derivative instruments that currently give the entity access to the returns.

14 IFRS 9 *Financial Instruments* does not apply to interests in associates and joint ventures that are accounted for using the equity method. When instruments containing potential voting rights in substance currently give access to the returns associated with an ownership interest in an associate or a joint venture, the instruments are not subject to IFRS 9. In all other cases, instruments containing potential voting rights in an associate or a joint venture are accounted for in accordance with IFRS 9.

15 Unless an investment, or a portion of an investment, in an associate or a joint venture is classified as held for sale in accordance with IFRS 5 *Non-current Assets Held for Sale and Discontinued Operations*, the investment, or any retained interest in the investment not classified as held for sale, shall be classified as a non-current asset.

Application of the equity method

16 An entity with joint control of, or significant influence over, an investee shall account for its investment in an associate or a joint venture using the equity method except when that investment qualifies for exemption in accordance with paragraphs 17 – 19.

Exemptions from applying the equity method

17 An entity need not apply the equity method to its investment in an associate or a joint

venture if the entity is a parent that is exempt from preparing consolidated financial statements by the scope exception in paragraph 4(a) of IFRS 10 or if all the following apply:

(a) The entity is a wholly-owned subsidiary, or is a partially-owned subsidiary of another entity and its other owners, including those not otherwise entitled to vote, have been informed about, and do not object to, the entity not applying the equity method.

(b) The entity's debt or equity instruments are not traded in a public market (a domestic or foreign stock exchange or an over-the-counter market, including local and regional markets).

(c) The entity did not file, nor is it in the process of filing, its financial statements with a securities commission or other regulatory organisation, for the purpose of issuing any class of instruments in a public market.

(d) The ultimate or any intermediate parent of the entity produces consolidated financial statements available for public use that comply with IFRSs.

18 When an investment in an associate or a joint venture is held by, or is held indirectly through, an entity that is a venture capital organisation, or a mutual fund, unit trust and similar entities including investment-linked insurance funds, the entity may elect to measure investments in those associates and joint ventures at fair value through profit or loss in accordance with IFRS 9.

19 When an entity has an investment in an associate, a portion of which is held indirectly through a venture capital organisation, or a mutual fund, unit trust and similar entities including investment-linked insurance funds, the entity may elect to measure that portion of the investment in the associate at fair value through profit or loss in accordance with IFRS 9 regardless of whether the venture capital organisation, or the mutual fund, unit trust and similar entities including investment-linked insurance funds, has significant influence over that portion of the investment. If the entity makes that election, the entity shall apply the equity method to any remaining portion of its investment in an associate that is not held through a venture capital organisation, or a mutual fund, unit trust and similar entities including investment-linked insurance funds.

Classification as held for sale

20 An entity shall apply IFRS 5 to an investment, or a portion of an investment, in an associate or a joint venture that meets the criteria to be classified as held for sale. Any

retained portion of an investment in an associate or a joint venture that has not been classified as held for sale shall be accounted for using the equity method until disposal of the portion that is classified as held for sale takes place. After the disposal takes place, an entity shall account for any retained interest in the associate or joint venture in accordance with IFRS 9 unless the retained interest continues to be an associate or a joint venture, in which case the entity uses the equity method.

21 When an investment, or a portion of an investment, in an associate or a joint venture previously classified as held for sale no longer meets the criteria to be so classified, it shall be accounted for using the equity method retrospectively as from the date of its classification as held for sale. Financial statements for the periods since classification as held for sale shall be amended accordingly.

Discontinuing the use of the equity method

22 **An entity shall discontinue the use of the equity method from the date when its investment ceases to be an associate or a joint venture as follows:**

(a) If the investment becomes a subsidiary, the entity shall account for its investment in accordance with IFRS 3 *Business Combinations* and IFRS 10.

(b) If the retained interest in the former associate or joint venture is a financial asset, the entity shall measure the retained interest at fair value. The fair value of the retained interest shall be regarded as its fair value on initial recognition as a financial asset in accordance with IFRS 9. The entity shall recognise in profit or loss any difference between:

(i) the fair value of any retained interest and any proceeds from disposing of a part interest in the associate or joint venture; and

(ii) the carrying amount of the investment at the date the equity method was discontinued.

(c) When an entity discontinues the use of the equity method, the entity shall account for all amounts previously recognised in other comprehensive income in relation to that investment on the same basis as would have been required if the investee had directly disposed of the related assets or liabilities.

23 **Therefore, if a gain or loss previously recognised in other comprehensive income by the investee would be reclassified to profit or loss on the disposal of the related assets or liabilities, the entity reclassifies the gain or loss from equity to profit or**

loss (as a reclassification adjustment) when the equity method is discontinued. For example, if an associate or a joint venture has cumulative exchange differences relating to a foreign operation and the entity discontinues the use of the equity method, the entity shall reclassify to profit or loss the gain or loss that had previously been recognised in other comprehensive income in relation to the foreign operation.

24 **If an investment in an associate becomes an investment in a joint venture or an investment in a joint venture becomes an investment in an associate, the entity continues to apply the equity method and does not remeasure the retained interest.**

Changes in ownership interest

25 If an entity's ownership interest in an associate or a joint venture is reduced, but the entity continues to apply the equity method, the entity shall reclassify to profit or loss the proportion of the gain or loss that had previously been recognised in other comprehensive income relating to that reduction in ownership interest if that gain or loss would be required to be reclassified to profit or loss on the disposal of the related assets or liabilities.

Equity method procedures

26 Many of the procedures that are appropriate for the application of the equity method are similar to the consolidation procedures described in IFRS 10. Furthermore, the concepts underlying the procedures used in accounting for the acquisition of a subsidiary are also adopted in accounting for the acquisition of an investment in an associate or a joint venture.

27 A group's share in an associate or a joint venture is the aggregate of the holdings in that associate or joint venture by the parent and its subsidiaries. The holdings of the group's other associates or joint ventures are ignored for this purpose. When an associate or a joint venture has subsidiaries, associates or joint ventures, the profit or loss, other comprehensive income and net assets taken into account in applying the equity method are those recognised in the associate's or joint venture's financial statements (including the associate's or joint venture's share of the profit or loss, other comprehensive income and net assets of its associates and joint ventures), after any adjustments necessary to give effect to uniform accounting policies (see paragraphs 35 and 36).

28 Gains and losses resulting from 'upstream' and 'downstream' transactions between an entity (including its consolidated subsidiaries) and its associate or joint venture are

recognised in the entity's financial statements only to the extent of unrelated investors' interests in the associate or joint venture. 'Upstream' transactions are, for example, sales of assets from an associate or a joint venture to the investor. 'Downstream' transactions are, for example, sales or contributions of assets from the investor to its associate or its joint venture. The investor's share in the associate's or joint venture's gains or losses resulting from these transactions is eliminated.

29 When downstream transactions provide evidence of a reduction in the net realisable value of the assets to be sold or contributed, or of an impairment loss of those assets, those losses shall be recognised in full by the investor. When upstream transactions provide evidence of a reduction in the net realisable value of the assets to be purchased or of an impairment loss of those assets, the investor shall recognise its share in those losses.

30 The contribution of a non-monetary asset to an associate or a joint venture in exchange for an equity interest in the associate or joint venture shall be accounted for in accordance with paragraph 28, except when the contribution lacks commercial substance, as that term is described in IAS 16 *Property, Plant and Equipment*. If such a contribution lacks commercial substance, the gain or loss is regarded as unrealised and is not recognised unless paragraph 31 also applies. Such unrealised gains and losses shall be eliminated against the investment accounted for using the equity method and shall not be presented as deferred gains or losses in the entity's consolidated statement of financial position or in the entity's statement of financial position in which investments are accounted for using the equity method.

31 If, in addition to receiving an equity interest in an associate or a joint venture, an entity receives monetary or non-monetary assets, the entity recognises in full in profit or loss the portion of the gain or loss on the non-monetary contribution relating to the monetary or non-monetary assets received.

32 An investment is accounted for using the equity method from the date on which it becomes an associate or a joint venture. On acquisition of the investment, any difference between the cost of the investment and the entity's share of the net fair value of the investee's identifiable assets and liabilities is accounted for as follows:

(a) Goodwill relating to an associate or a joint venture is included in the carrying amount of the investment. Amortisation of that goodwill is not permitted.

(b) Any excess of the entity's share of the net fair value of the investee's identifiable assets and liabilities over the cost of the investment is included as income in the determination of the entity's share of the associate or joint venture's profit or loss in the period in which the investment is acquired.

Appropriate adjustments to the entity's share of the associate's or joint venture's profit or loss after acquisition are made in order to account, for example, for depreciation of the depreciable assets based on their fair values at the acquisition date. Similarly, appropriate adjustments to the entity's share of the associate's or joint venture's profit or loss after acquisition are made for impairment losses such as for goodwill or property, plant and equipment.

33 **The most recent available financial statements of the associate or joint venture are used by the entity in applying the equity method. When the end of the reporting period of the entity is different from that of the associate or joint venture, the associate or joint venture prepares, for the use of the entity, financial statements as of the same date as the financial statements of the entity unless it is impracticable to do so.**

34 **When, in accordance with paragraph 33, the financial statements of an associate or a joint venture used in applying the equity method are prepared as of a date different from that used by the entity, adjustments shall be made for the effects of significant transactions or events that occur between that date and the date of the entity's financial statements. In any case, the difference between the end of the reporting period of the associate or joint venture and that of the entity shall be no more than three months. The length of the reporting periods and any difference between the ends of the reporting periods shall be the same from period to period.**

35 **The entity's financial statements shall be prepared using uniform accounting policies for like transactions and events in similar circumstances.**

36 If an associate or a joint venture uses accounting policies other than those of the entity for like transactions and events in similar circumstances, adjustments shall be made to make the associate's or joint venture's accounting policies conform to those of the entity when the associate's or joint venture's financial statements are used by the entity in applying the equity method.

37 If an associate or a joint venture has outstanding cumulative preference shares that are held by parties other than the entity and are classified as equity, the entity computes its share of profit or loss after adjusting for the dividends on such shares, whether or not the dividends have been declared.

38 If an entity's share of losses of an associate or a joint venture equals or exceeds its interest in the associate or joint venture, the entity discontinues recognising its share of

further losses. The interest in an associate or a joint venture is the carrying amount of the investment in the associate or joint venture determined using the equity method together with any long-term interests that, in substance, form part of the entity's net investment in the associate or joint venture. For example, an item for which settlement is neither planned nor likely to occur in the foreseeable future is, in substance, an extension of the entity's investment in that associate or joint venture. Such items may include preference shares and l ong-term receivables or loans, but do not include trade receivables, trade payables or any long-term receivables for which adequate collateral exists, such as secured loans. Losses recognised using the equity method in excess of the entity's investment in ordinary shares are applied to the other components of the entity's interest in an associate or a joint venture in the reverse order of their seniority (ie priority in liquidation).

39 After the entity's interest is reduced to zero, additional losses are provided for, and a liability is recognised, only to the extent that the entity has incurred legal or constructive obligations or made payments on behalf of the associate or joint venture. If the associate or joint venture subsequently reports profits, the entity resumes recognising its share of those profits only after its share of the profits equals the share of losses not recognised.

Impairment losses

40 After application of the equity method, including recognising the associate's or joint venture's losses in accordance with paragraph 38, the entity applies IAS 39 *Financial Instruments: Recognition and Measurement* to determine whether it is necessary to recognise any additional impairment loss with respect to its net investment in the associate or joint venture.

41 The entity also applies IAS 39 to determine whether any additional impairment loss is recognised with respect to its interest in the associate or joint venture that does not constitute part of the net investment and the amount of that impairment loss.

42 Because goodwill that forms part of the carrying amount of an investment in an associate or a joint venture is not separately recognised, it is not tested for impairment separately by applying the requirements for impairment testing goodwill in IAS 36 *Impairment of Assets*. Instead, the entire carrying amount of the investment is tested for impairment in accordance with IAS 36 as a single asset, by comparing its recoverable amount (higher of value in use and fair value less costs to sell) with its carrying amount, whenever application of IAS 39 indicates that the investment may be impaired. An impairment loss recognised in those circumstances is not allocated to any asset, including goodwill, that forms part of the carrying amount of the investment in the associate or joint venture.

Accordingly, any reversal of that impairment loss is recognised in accordance with IAS 36 to the extent that the recoverable amount of the investment subsequently increases. In determining the value in use of the investment, an entity estimates:

(a) its share of the present value of the estimated future cash flows expected to be generated by the associate or joint venture, including the cash flows from the operations of the associate or joint venture and the proceeds from the ultimate disposal of the investment; or

(b) the present value of the estimated future cash flows expected to arise from dividends to be received from the investment and from its ultimate disposal.

Using appropriate assumptions, both methods give the same result.

43 The recoverable amount of an investment in an associate or a joint venture shall be assessed for each associate or joint venture, unless the associate or joint venture does not generate cash inflows from continuing use that are largely independent of those from other assets of the entity.

Separate financial statements

44 An investment in an associate or a joint venture shall be accounted for in the entity's separate financial statements in accordance with paragraph 10 of IAS 27 (as amended in 2011).

Effective date and transition

45 An entity shall apply this Standard for annual periods beginning on or after 1 January 2013. Earlier application is permitted. If an entity applies this Standard earlier, it shall disclose that fact and apply IFRS 10, IFRS 11 *Joint Arrangements*, IFRS 12 *Disclosure of Interests in Other Entities* and IAS 27 (as amended in 2011) at the same time.

References to IFRS 9

46 If an entity applies this Standard but does not yet apply IFRS 9, any reference to IFRS 9 shall be read as a reference to IAS 39.

Withdrawal of IAS 28 (2003)

47 This Standard supersedes IAS 28 *Investments in Associates* (as revised in 2003).

Approval by the Board of IAS 28 issued in December 2003

International Accounting Standard 28 *Investments in Associates* (as revised in 2003) was approved for issue by the fourteen members of the International Accounting Standards Board.

Sir David Tweedie	Chairman
Thomas E Jones	Vice-Chairman
Mary E Barth	
Hans-Georg Bruns	
Anthony T Cope	
Robert P Garnett	
Gilbert Gélard	
James J Leisenring	
Warren J McGregor	
Patricia L O'Malley	
Harry K Schmid	
John T Smith	
Geoffrey Whittington	
Tatsumi Yamada	

Basis for Conclusions on IAS 28 *Investments in Associates and Joint Ventures*

This Basis for Conclusions accompanies, but is not part of, IAS 28.

Introduction

BC1 This Basis for Conclusions summarises the International Accounting Standards Board's considerations in reaching its conclusions on amending IAS 28 *Investments in Associates* in 2011. Individual Board members gave greater weight to some factors than to others.

BC2 The amendment of IAS 28 resulted from the Board's project on joint ventures. When discussing that project, the Board decided to incorporate the accounting for joint ventures into IAS 28 because the equity method is applicable to both joint ventures and associates.

BC3 As a result, the title of IAS 28 was changed to *Investments in Associates and Joint Ventures*. Because the Board's intention was not to reconsider the fundamental approach to the accounting for investments in associates established by IAS 28, the Board has incorporated into its Basis for Conclusions on IAS 28 material from the Basis for Conclusions on IAS 28 (as revised in 2003) that the Board has not reconsidered.

The structure of IAS 28 and the Board's deliberations

BC4 IAS 28 as amended in 2011 superseded IAS 28 (as revised in 2003 and amended in 2010). As stated in paragraph BC3, in amending IAS 28, the Board did not reconsider all the Standard's requirements. The requirements in paragraphs 5-11, 15, 22-23, 25-28 and 32-43 relate to the assessment of significant influence and to the equity method and its application, and paragraphs 12-14 relate to the accounting for potential voting rights. With the exception of the Board's decision to incorporate the accounting for joint ventures into IAS 28, those paragraphs were carried forward from IAS 28 and from the Guidance on Implementing IAS 27 *Consolidated and Separate Financial Statements*, IAS 28 *Investments in Associates* and IAS 31 *Interests in Joint Ventures* that was withdrawn when IFRS 10 *Consolidated Financial Statements*, IFRS 11 *Joint Arrangements* and IAS 28 (as amended in 2011) were issued. As a result, those paragraphs were not reconsidered by the Board.

BC5 When revised in 2003 IAS 28 was accompanied by a Basis for Conclusions summarising the considerations of the Board, as constituted at the time, in reaching its conclusions. That Basis for Conclusions was subsequently updated to reflect amendments to the

Standard.

BC6 The Board has incorporated into its Basis for Conclusions on IAS 28 (as amended in 2011) material from the previous Basis for Conclusions because it discusses matters that the Board has not reconsidered. That material is contained in paragraphs denoted by numbers with the prefix BCZ. In those paragraphs cross-references have been updated accordingly and minor necessary editorial changes have been made.

BC7 One Board member dissented from an amendment to IAS 28 issued in May 2008, which has been carried forward to IAS 28 (as amended in 2011). His dissenting opinion is also set out after this Basis for Conclusions.

BC8 The requirements in paragraphs 2, 16-21, 24 and 29-31 relate to matters addressed within the joint ventures project that led to amendments to IAS 28. Paragraphs describing the Board's considerations in reaching its conclusions on IAS 28 are numbered with the prefix BC.

BC9 As part of its project on consolidation, the Board is examining how an investment entity accounts for its interests in subsidiaries, joint ventures and associates. The outcome might affect how organisations such as venture capital organisations, or mutual funds, unit trusts and similar entities account for their interests in joint ventures and associates. The Board expects to publish later in 2011 an exposure draft on investment entities.

Scope

BC10 During its redeliberation of the exposure draft ED 9 *Joint Arrangements*, the Board reconsidered the scope exception of IAS 31 that had also been proposed in ED 9. The Board concluded that the scope exception in ED 9 for interests in joint ventures held by venture capital organisations, or mutual funds, unit trusts and similar entities, including investment-linked insurance funds, that are measured at fair value through profit or loss in accordance with IFRS 9 *Financial Instruments* is more appropriately characterised as a measurement exemption, and not as a scope exception.

BC11 The Board observed that IAS 28 had a similar scope exception for investments in associates held by venture capital organisations, or mutual funds, unit trusts and similar entities, including investment-linked insurance funds, that are measured at fair value through profit or loss in accordance with IFRS 9.

BC12 The Board observed that the scope exception in ED 9 and IAS 28 related not to the fact that these arrangements do not have the characteristics of joint arrangements or those investments are not associates, but to the fact that for investments held by venture capital organisations, or mutual funds, unit trusts and similar entities including investment-linked insurance funds, fair value measurement provides more useful information for users of the financial statements than would application of the equity method.

BC13 Accordingly, the Board decided to maintain the option that permits venture capital organisations, or mutual funds, unit trusts and similar entities including investment-linked insurance funds to measure their interests in joint ventures and associates at fair value through profit or loss in accordance with IFRS 9, but clarified that this is an exemption from the requirement to measure interests in joint ventures and associates using the equity method, rather than an exception to the scope of IAS 28 for the accounting for joint ventures and associates held by those entities.

BC14 As a result of that decision and of the decision to incorporate the accounting for joint ventures into IAS 28, the Board decided that IAS 28 should be applied to the accounting for investments held by all entities that have joint control of, or significant influence over, an investee.

Significant influence

Potential voting rights

BC15 In its deliberation of the amendments to IAS 28, the Board considered whether the requirements now in paragraphs 7-9 of IAS 28 regarding potential voting rights when assessing significant influence should be changed to be consistent with the requirements developed in the consolidation project.

BC16 The Board observed that the definition of significant influence in IAS 28 (ie 'the power to participate in the financial and operating policy decisions of the investee but is not control or joint control of those policies') was related to the definition of control as it was defined in IAS 27. The Board had not considered the definition of significant influence when it amended IAS 28 and concluded that it would not be appropriate to change one element of significant influence in isolation. Any such consideration should be done as part of a wider review of the accounting for associates.

Application of the equity method

Temporary joint control and significant influence (2003 revision)

BCZ17 In IFRS 5 *Non-current Assets Held for Sale and Discontinued Operations* the Board decided not to exempt an entity from applying the equity method for accounting for its investments in joint ventures and associates when joint control of, or significant influence over, an investee is intended to be temporary.

Severe long-term restrictions impairing ability to transfer funds to the investor (2003 revision)

BCZ18 The Board decided not to exempt an entity from applying the equity method for accounting for its investments in joint ventures or associates when severe long-term restrictions impaired a joint venture or an associate's ability to transfer funds to the investor. It did so because such circumstances may not preclude the entity's joint control of, or significant influence over, the joint venture or the associate. The Board decided that an entity should, when assessing its ability to exercise joint control of, or significant influence over, an investee, consider restrictions on the transfer of funds from the joint venture or from the associate to the entity. In themselves, such restrictions do not preclude the existence of joint control or significant influence.

Non-coterminous year-ends (2003 revision)

BCZ19 The exposure draft that preceded the revision of IAS 28 in 2003 proposed to limit to three months any difference between the reporting dates of an entity and its associate or its joint venture when applying the equity method. Some respondents to that exposure draft believed that it could be impracticable for the entity to prepare financial statements as of the same date when the date of the entity's financial statements and those of the associate or joint venture differ by more than three months. The Board noted that a three-month limit operates in several jurisdictions and it was concerned that a longer period, such as six months, would lead to the recognition of stale information. Therefore, it decided to retain the three-month limit.

Exemptions from applying the equity method: partial use of fair value measurement of associates

BC20 The Board received a request to clarify whether different measurement bases can be applied to portions of an investment in an associate when part of the investment is not accounted for using the equity method in accordance with paragraph 18 of IAS 28, but it is instead measured at fair value through profit or loss in accordance with IFRS 9. The Board initially deliberated this amendment to IAS 28 as part of the *Improvements to IFRSs* issued in April 2010; however, at its meeting in February 2010 the Board decided to address this issue within the joint ventures project.

BC21 The Board noted that two views exist with respect to measurement. The first view identifies all direct and indirect interests held in the associate either by the parent or through any of its subsidiaries, and then applies IAS 28 to the entire investment in the associate. In accordance with this view, there is only one investment in the associate and it should be accounted for as a single unit. The second view identifies all direct and indirect interests held in an associate, but then allows the use of the measurement exemption to portions of an investment in an associate if the portion is held by a venture capital organisation, or a mutual fund, unit trust and similar entities including investment-linked insurance funds, regardless of whether those entities have significant influence over their portion of the investment in the associate. The Board agreed with the second view and therefore amended IAS 28. The Board decided that equivalent guidance on the partial use of fair value for the measurement of investments in joint ventures should not be provided because the Board thought that such events would be unlikely in practice.

BC22 The Board also discussed whether the partial use of fair value should be allowed only in the case of venture capital organisations, or mutual funds, unit trusts and similar entities including investment-linked insurance funds, that have designated their portion of the investment in the associate at fair value through profit or loss in their own financial statements. The Board noted that several situations might arise in which those entities do not measure their portion of the investment in the associate at fair value through profit or loss. In those situations, however, from the group's perspective, the appropriate determination of the business purpose would lead to the measurement of this portion of the investment in the associate at fair value through profit or loss in the consolidated financial statements. Consequently, the Board decided that an entity should be able to measure a portion of an investment in an associate held by a venture capital organisation, or a mutual fund, unit trust and similar entities including investment-linked insurance funds, at fair value through profit or loss regardless of whether this portion of the investment is measured at fair value through profit or loss in those entities' financial statements.

Classification as held for sale

BC23 ED 9 proposed that an entity should account for an interest in a joint venture that is classified as held for sale in accordance with IFRS 5.

BC24 During its redeliberation of ED 9 the Board noted that the exposure draft *Improvements to IFRSs* published in August 2009 had proposed to amend IFRS 5 so as to require an entity to classify as held for sale its interest in an associate, or in a jointly controlled entity, when it is committed to a sale plan involving loss of significant influence or loss of joint control. Those proposals aimed to clarify that all the interest ('the whole interest') an entity had in an associate or a joint venture had to be classified as held for sale if the entity was committed to a sale plan involving loss of, significant influence over, or joint control of that interest.

BC25 The Board observed that those proposals were not aligned with the decisions made during the Board's redeliberation of ED 9 to remove all descriptions that associated the loss of joint control and the loss of significant influence with the term 'significant economic event' as introduced in the second phase of the Board's project on business combinations (see paragraphs BC28-BC31).

BC26 The Board decided that classifying an interest as held for sale should be on the basis of whether the intended disposal meets the criteria for classification as held for sale in accordance with IFRS 5, rather than on whether the entity had lost joint control of, or significant influence over, that interest. As a result, the Board concluded that when the disposal of an interest, or a portion of an interest, in a joint venture or an associate fulfilled the criteria for classification as held for sale in accordance with IFRS 5, an entity should classify the whole interest, or a portion of the interest, as held for sale.

BC27 The Board decided that, in the case of a partial disposal, an entity should maintain the use of the equity method for the retained interest in the joint venture or associate until the portion classified as held for sale is finally disposed of. The Board reasoned that even if the entity has the intention of selling a portion of an interest in an associate or a joint venture, until it does so it still has significant influence over, or joint control of, that investee. After the disposal, an entity should measure the retained interest in the joint venture or associate in accordance with IFRS 9 or in accordance with IAS 28 if the entity still has significant influence over, or joint control of, the retained interest.

Discontinuing the use of the equity method

BC28 During its redeliberation of ED 9, the Board reconsidered whether its decision in the second phase of the business combinations project to characterise loss of joint control or loss of significant influence as a significant economic event (ie in the same way that loss of control is characterised as a significant economic event) was appropriate. If it were, the Board thought that the entity should be required to recalibrate the accounting as required by IFRS 10. However, the Board concluded that, although significant, the events are fundamentally different. In the case of loss of control, the cessation of the parent-subsidiary relationship results in the derecognition of assets and liabilities because the composition of the group changes. If joint control or significant influence is lost the composition of the group is unaffected.

BC29 The Board also noted that retaining the characterisation of significant economic event in the case of loss of joint control or significant influence when the retained interest is a financial asset is unnecessary. IFRS 9 already requires that in such cases the retained interest (ie a financial asset) must be measured at fair value.

BC30 In the case of loss of joint control when significant influence is maintained, the Board acknowledged that the investor-investee relationship changes and, consequently, so does the nature of the investment. However, in this instance, both investments (ie the joint venture and the associate) continue to be measured using the equity method. Considering that there is neither a change in the group boundaries nor a change in the measurement requirements, the Board concluded that losing joint control and retaining significant influence is not an event that warrants remeasurement of the retained interest at fair value.

BC31 Consequently, the Board removed all descriptions that characterise loss of joint control or significant influence as a significant economic event as introduced in the second phase of the Board's project on business combinations.

Incorporation of SIC-13

BC32 In the joint ventures project, the Board decided to extend the requirements and guidance in IAS 28 for the accounting for 'downstream' and 'upstream' transactions between an entity and its associate to the accounting for transactions between an entity and its joint venture.

BC33 In ED 9, the Board proposed to incorporate into the standard on joint arrangements the consensus of SIC-13 *Jointly Controlled Entities—Non-Monetary Contributions by Venturers*. Because the Board relocated all the requirements for the accounting for joint ventures into IAS 28, the Board incorporated the consensus of SIC-13 into IAS 28 and extended it to associates.

BC34 The Board noted that the consensus of SIC-13 regarding non-monetary contributions made by a venturer[1] to a joint venture is consistent with IAS 28, except for the following aspect. SIC-13 established three exceptions for the recognition of gains or losses attributable to the equity interests of the other parties. In response to comments raised by some respondents to ED 9, the Board redeliberated the need to incorporate into IAS 28 the exceptions included in SIC-13 for the recognition by an entity of the portion of a gain or loss attributable to the interests of other unrelated investors in the investee.

BC35 The Board concluded that only when the transaction lacks commercial substance should there be an exception for the recognition of gains or losses to be carried forward from the consensus of SIC-13 into IAS 28, because the other two exceptions in SIC-13 (ie 'the significant risks and rewards of ownership of the contributed non-monetary asset(s) have not been transferred to the jointly controlled entity' and 'the gain or loss on the non-monetary contribution cannot be measured reliably') either relate to requirements that are not aligned with the principles and requirements of IFRS 11 or relate to a criterion for the recognition of gain or losses (ie 'reliability of measurement') that is already included in the *Conceptual Framework for Financial Reporting*.

BCZ36 To the extent that the entity also receives monetary or non-monetary assets dissimilar to the assets contributed in addition to equity interests in the investee, the realisation of which is not dependent on the future cash flows of the investee, the earnings process is complete. Accordingly, an entity should recognise in full in profit or loss the portion of the gain or loss on the non-monetary contribution relating to the monetary or non-monetary assets received.

BC37 Additionally, the Board considered whether the requirements in IAS 31 for recognition of losses when downstream or upstream transactions provide evidence of a reduction in the net realisable value or impairment loss of the assets transacted or contributed were still relevant and decided to bring them forward to IAS 28.

Recognition of losses (2003 revision)

BCZ38 The 2000 version of IAS 28 and SIC-20 *Equity Accounting Method—Recognition of Losses* restricted application of the equity method when, in accounting for the entity's share of losses, the carrying amount of the investment is reduced to zero.

BCZ39 The Board decided that the base to be reduced to zero should be broader than residual equity interests and should also include other non-equity interests that are in substance

[1] IFRS 11 *Joint Arrangements*, issued in May 2011, uses the term 'joint venturers' to designate parties that have joint control of a joint venture.

part of the net investment in the associate or joint venture, such as long-term receivables. Therefore, the Board decided to withdraw SIC-20.

BCZ40 The Board also noted that if non-equity investments are not included in the base to be reduced to zero, an entity could restructure its investment to fund the majority in non-equity investments to avoid recognising the losses of the associate or joint venture under the equity method.

BCZ41 In widening the base against which losses are to be recognised, the Board also clarified the application of the impairment provisions of IAS 39 *Financial Instruments: Recognition and Measurement* to the financial assets that form part of the net investment.

Impairment losses (2008 amendment)

BCZ42 In 2008 the Board identified unclear guidance in IAS 28 regarding the extent to which an impairment reversal should be recognised as an adjustment to the carrying amount of an investment in an associate or in a joint venture.

BCZ43 The Board noted that applying the equity method involves adjusting the entity's share of the impairment loss recognised by the associate or joint venture on assets such as goodwill or property, plant and equipment to take account of the acquisition date fair values of those assets. The Board proposed in the exposure draft *Improvements to International Financial Reporting Standards* published in October 2007 that an additional impairment recognised by the entity, after applying the equity method, should not be allocated to any asset, including goodwill, that forms part of the carrying amount of the investment. Therefore, such an impairment should be reversed in a subsequent period to the extent that the recoverable amount of the investment increases.

BCZ44 Some respondents to the exposure draft expressed the view that the proposed amendment was not consistent with IAS 39 (regarding reversal of an impairment loss on an available-for-sale equity instrument), or with IAS 36 *Impairment of Assets* (regarding the allocation of an impairment loss to goodwill and any reversal of an impairment loss relating to goodwill).

BCZ45 In its redeliberations, the Board affirmed its previous decisions but, in response to the comments made, decided to clarify the reasons for the amendments. The Board decided that an entity should not allocate an impairment loss to any asset that forms part of the carrying amount of the investment in the associate or joint venture because the investment is the only asset that the entity controls and recognises.

BCZ46 The Board also decided that any reversal of this impairment loss should be recognised as an adjustment to the investment in the associate or joint venture to the extent that the recoverable amount of the investment increases. This requirement is consistent with IAS 36, which permits the reversal of impairment losses for assets other than goodwill. The Board did not propose to align the requirements for the reversal of an impairment loss with those in IAS 39 relating to equity instruments, because an entity recognises an impairment loss on an investment in an associate or joint venture in accordance with IAS 36, rather than in accordance with IAS 39.

Effective date and transition

BC47 The Board decided to align the effective date for the Standard with the effective date for IFRS 10, IFRS 11, IFRS 12 *Disclosure of Interests in Other Entities* and IAS 27 *Separate Financial Statements*. When making this decision, the Board noted that the five IFRSs all deal with the assessment of, and related accounting and disclosure requirements about, a reporting entity's special relationships with other entities (ie when the reporting entity has control or joint control of, or significant influence over, another entity). As a result, the Board concluded that applying IAS 28 without also applying the other four IFRSs could cause unwarranted confusion.

BC48 The Board usually sets an effective date of between twelve and eighteen months after issuing an IFRS. When deciding the effective date for those IFRSs, the Board considered the following factors:

(a) the time that many countries require for translation and for introducing the mandatory requirements into law.

(b) the consolidation project was related to the global financial crisis that started in 2007 and was accelerated by the Board in response to urgent requests from the leaders of the G20, the Financial Stability Board, users of financial statements, regulators and others to improve the accounting and disclosure of an entity's 'off balance sheet' activities.

(c) the comments received from respondents to the Request for Views *Effective Date and Transition Methods* that was published in October 2010 regarding implementation costs, effective date and transition requirements of the IFRSs to be issued in 2011. Most respondents did not identify the consolidation and joint arrangements IFRSs as having a high impact in terms of the time and resources that their implementation would require. In addition, only a few respondents commented that the effective dates of those IFRSs should be aligned with those of the other IFRSs to be issued in 2011.

BC49 With those factors in mind, the Board decided to require entities to apply the five IFRSs for annual periods beginning on or after 1 January 2013.

BC50 Most respondents to the Request for Views supported early application of the IFRSs to be issued in 2011. Respondents stressed that early application was especially important for first-time adopters in 2011 and 2012. The Board was persuaded by these arguments and decided to permit early application of IAS 28 but only if an entity applies it in conjunction with the other IFRSs (ie IFRS 10, IFRS 11, IFRS 12 and IAS 27 (as amended in 2011)) to avoid a lack of comparability among financial statements, and for the reasons noted in paragraph BC47 that triggered the Board's decision to set the same effective date for all five IFRSs. Even though an entity should apply the five IFRSs at the same time, the Board noted that an entity should not be prevented from providing any information required by IFRS 12 early if by doing so users gained a better understanding of the entity's relationships with other entities.

General

Withdrawal of IAS 28 (2003 revision)

BC51 IAS 28 *Investments in Associates and Joint Ventures* replaces IAS 28 *Investments in Associates* (as revised in 2003 and amended in 2010). IAS 28 (as amended in 2011) incorporates the accounting for joint ventures and includes some amendments discussed by the Board during its redeliberation of the exposure draft ED 9.

Disclosure

BC52 IAS 28 does not address the disclosure requirements for entities with joint control of, or significant influence over, an investee. As part of its redeliberation of ED 9 and ED 10 *Consolidated Financial Statements*, the Board identified an opportunity to integrate and make consistent the disclosure requirements for subsidiaries, joint arrangements, associates and unconsolidated structured entities, and to present those requirements in a single IFRS.

BC53 The Board observed that IAS 27, IAS 28 and IAS 31 contained many similar disclosure requirements. ED 9 had already proposed amendments to the disclosure requirements for joint ventures and associates to align the disclosure requirements for those two types of investments more closely. The Board noted that the majority of respondents agreed with the proposals in ED 9 to align the disclosures for joint ventures with the disclosures in IAS 28 for associates.

BC54 As a result, the Board combined the disclosure requirements for interest with subsidiaries, joint arrangements, associates and unconsolidated structured entities within a single comprehensive standard, IFRS 12.

BC55 The Basis for Conclusions accompanying IFRS 12 summarises the Board's considerations in developing that IFRS, including its review of responses to the disclosure proposals in ED 9. Accordingly, IAS 28 does not include disclosure requirements and this Basis for Conclusions does not incorporate the Board's considerations of responses to the proposed disclosure requirements in ED 9.

Summary of main changes from IAS 28 (2003 revision)

BC56 The main changes from the previous version of IAS 28 are as follows:

(a) The accounting for joint ventures has been incorporated into the Standard.

(b) The scope exception for venture capital organisations, or mutual funds, unit trusts and similar entities, including investment-linked insurance funds has been eliminated and has been characterised as a measurement exemption from the requirement to measure investments in associates and joint ventures in using the equity method.

(c) IAS 28 now permits an entity that has an investment in an associate, a portion of which is held indirectly through venture capital organisations, or mutual funds, unit trusts and similar entities including investment-linked insurance funds, to elect to measure that portion of the investment in the associate at fair value through profit or loss in accordance with IFRS 9 regardless of whether these entities have significant influence over that portion of the investment.

(d) IAS 28 requires a portion of an investment in an associate or a joint venture to be classified as held for sale if the disposal of that portion of the interest would fulfil the criteria to be classified as held for sale in accordance with IFRS 5.

(e) The consensus of SIC-13 has been incorporated into IAS 28. As a result, gains and losses resulting from a contribution of a non-monetary asset to an associate or a joint venture in exchange for an equity interest in an associate or a joint venture are recognised only to the extent of unrelated investors' interests in the associate or joint venture, except when the contribution lacks commercial substance, as that term is described in IAS 16 *Property, Plant and Equipment*.

(f) The disclosure requirements have been placed in IFRS 12.

DISSENTING OPINION

Dissenting opinion on amendment issued in May 2008

Dissent of Tatsumi Yamada

DO1 Mr Yamada voted against one of the amendments to IAS 28 *Investments in Associates* issued in *Improvements to IFRSs* in May 2008.

DO2 Mr Yamada believes it is inappropriate not to allocate any additional impairment losses to the goodwill and other assets that form part of the carrying amount of the investment in the associate. In his view, because he believes that an investor can identify attributable goodwill when it makes an investment, all impairment losses recognised with respect to the investor's investment in an associate should be allocated to the goodwill and other assets that form part of the carrying amount of the investment.

DO3 Mr Yamada also believes that all impairment losses allocated to goodwill should not be subsequently reversed. In his view the non-allocation of impairment losses to goodwill as required by the amendment and the subsequent reversal of such impairment losses in substance leads to the recognition of internally generated goodwill. He believes that the amendment to IAS 28 is not consistent with paragraphs 124 and 125 of IAS 36 *Impairment of Assets* , which prohibit the reversal of impairment losses related to goodwill.

TABLE OF CONCORDANCE

This table shows how the contents of the superseded version of IAS 28 (as revised in 2003) and the amended version of IAS 28 in 2011 correspond. Some requirements in the superseded version of IAS 28 were incorporated into IFRS 12 *Disclosure of Interests in Other Entities*; this table also shows how those paragraphs correspond. Paragraphs are treated as corresponding if they broadly address the same matter even though the guidance may differ.

Superseded IAS 28 paragraph	Amended IAS 28 paragraph	IFRS 12 paragraph	Amended IAS 27 paragraph
1	2, 18, 19		
2	3, 4		
3			7
4			6
5			8
6	5		
7	6		
8	7		
9	8		
10	9		
11	10		
12	12		
13	17		
14	20		
15	21		
17	11		
18	22		

Superseded IAS 28 paragraph	Amended IAS 28 paragraph	IFRS 12 paragraph	Amended IAS 27 paragraph
19	22		
19A	23		
20	26		
21	27		
22	28		
23	32		
24	33		
25	34		
26	35		
27	36		
28	37		
29	38		
30	39		
31	40		
32	41		
33	42		
34	43		
35	44		
36			3
37		21-24	
38		21-24	
39		21-24	

Superseded IAS 28 paragraph	Amended IAS 28 paragraph	IFRS 12 paragraph	Amended IAS 27 paragraph
40		21-24	
41	45		
41A-41E			
42	47		
43	47		
None	1, 13-16, 24, 25, 29-31, 46		